On this date

November 24, 2001

(Birthday)

a **Guardian Angel**

was assigned to the Wonder Window of

Ki-Re Anna Klettke

(Name)

for guidance, love, and protection
throughout the journey of life.

Illustrated by Martha-Elizabeth Ferguson.

ISBN: 0-9634910-7-5

Library of Congress Card Number: 2001088274

10 9 8 7 6 5 4 3 2 1 First Edition March 2002

Printed in China

My Guardian Angel

Samara Anjelae

To Matthew and Jessie

BelleTress Books

Ask an angel to come into your life. The moment you ask is the moment your angel arrives. Guardian Angels are assigned at birth to every soul born. They come from the realm of heaven, where a pure source of love exists for all. When you open a window to your heart, even for an instant, you will find your Guardian Angel.

The word angel comes from the Greek word angelos, meaning messenger. Angels are thought of as messengers between God and humanity. The spirit of sharing, caring and communicating is part of the divine plan, a pattern of oneness among all created things.

Give your Guardian Angel a name or your angel may have already given the name to you. The name could come when you are singing, playing, or just being very still. Call the name when you are in the mood to talk to your special friend or when you want some love and guidance from your angel.

Make an angel a lifelong friend, messenger and companion.

Since the dawn of time, angels have graced us with their presence. Many cultures throughout the world believe in angels. Angels can come to us as:

Glowing beings
Pink balls of sparks
Helping spirits
Beams of light
Tingles on the neck
Sweet, unexplained smells
Intuition (a knowing)

Everybody experiences angels in their own special ways. These messengers bridge heaven and earth. They remind us of truth, beauty and goodness.

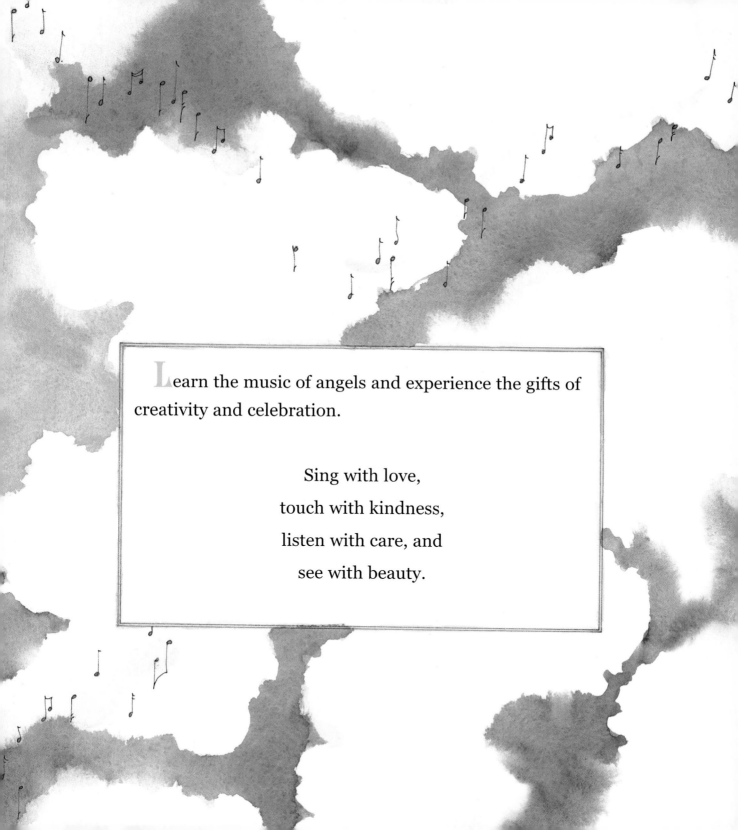

Learn the music of angels and experience the gifts of creativity and celebration.

Sing with love,

touch with kindness,

listen with care, and

see with beauty.

Special Sayings for the Week

Monday	Angel, Angel, come fly with me.
Tuesday	Help me make my day cheery and free.
Wednesday	Angel, Angel, bring me the best.
Thursday	Show me the way with all my tasks.
Friday	Angel, Angel, come create with me.
Saturday	Let's play throughout the day.
Sunday	Angel, Angel, let's say thanks and take a rest.

ake an imaginary walk. You may be in the woods, by the ocean, on a mountain, or at your home. Let your angel greet you as you wander. Next, imagine your heavenly friend handing you a gift. This gift or talent is one you already have but may have forgotten. Thank your angel for bringing you this idea that will help you become the best you can be. We are never given a hope or wish without also being given the opportunities to make it come true. As you grow, your gifts may change. Be aware of what your talents and dreams are today. There are no limits to creativity when angels inspire us. We just have to develop the ability to listen to our angels of inspiration.

GUARDIAN ANGEL ALPHABET

G is for Guidance that your angels bring.

U is for Understanding their soft messages.

A is for Always knowing that you are loved.

R is for Receiving angel blessings.

D is for Donating your toys or time to help others.

I is for Inspiring others to do the same.

A is for Appreciating the wonders of heaven.

N is for Noble acts that angels do.

A is for Accepting that everyone has a Guardian Angel.

N is for Never forgetting that angels are in your life.

G is for Giving your attention to kind thoughts.

E is for Enjoying your family and friends.

L is for Loving yourself,

Loving others and

Loving your

GUARDIAN ANGEL

If you need some love or want to love others more, call upon the Angel of Love. The Angel of Love teaches us to have deep and tender feelings of affection for others and for ourselves. Nurture the love in your heart, and share the love with others.

When you are feeling especially lonely and want some company, call upon the Angel of Friendship. The Angel of Friendship is ready to be a true friend – supportive, kind, considerate and respectful.

If you are having trouble being a good friend to others, ask the Angel of Friendship for guidance. This friendly angel is a never-ending source of goodwill, and is always available to help you spread your wings of kindness and acceptance.

Have you ever felt misunderstood or felt you were treated unfairly? The Angel of Fairness will help you honor your feelings, see a problem clearly, keep you honest and understand the actions of others. In time, the truth will be heard. All will come right and all will be well.

When you want to have fun, call upon the Angel of Play. This festive angel will make you smile, laugh and shine with light. Be ready to dance, skip, sing, and be filled with wonder. The Angel of Play brings good fortune, and is always inventing new ways to spread joy and happiness.

Celebrate Angels Every Month

January   Tell the first person you see every morning that you love them. Start by saying an angel hello, *"halo."*

February   Make snow or sand angels, and on a heartfelt day make your angel a valentine.

March   Find a four-leaf angelic clover and make a happy wish.

April   Write a poem about angels. Sing it to your angelic friends as they smile with delight.

May   Joyfully take some crayons or paints and draw a picture of your Guardian Angel. Watch your angel come alive.

June   Give your angel a treat. Make it nice and sweet. A big smile. An open heart. A happy halo. A kind word. A positive thought. A make-believe hug and a bite of your ice cream!

July	Be extra kind to all living creatures. Adopt, love, or care for a nearby animal. Try to see the world through the eyes of your animal friend.
August	On your back lie in the grass and find angels in the clouds.
September	Try to find the meaning of your name. The word angel means messenger. Know that you too are a messenger. Spread happiness this month.
October	Make something with your hands. While you create ask your angels to put their hands over yours.
November	Say a Prayer of Thanks. Enjoy your many blessings.
December	Leave out angel treats – plants, flowers, fragrances, beautiful cloths, peaceful music and best of all, your love.

When you are trying to figure out the difference between right and wrong, ask yourself, "What would an angel do in my same place?" When you have an answer, then carry on as an angel would.

In your heart you have hopes, wishes and concerns. When you pray you are sharing these thoughts. There are many ways to pray. Prayers are personal. You can pray alone or with others. You can pray to give thanks, ask for answers or ask for help. You can pray by singing, dancing, chanting, thinking, or even writing a poem.

God is my protector,
God is my light,
God is with me
Every day and night.
In this moment, I have all that I need.

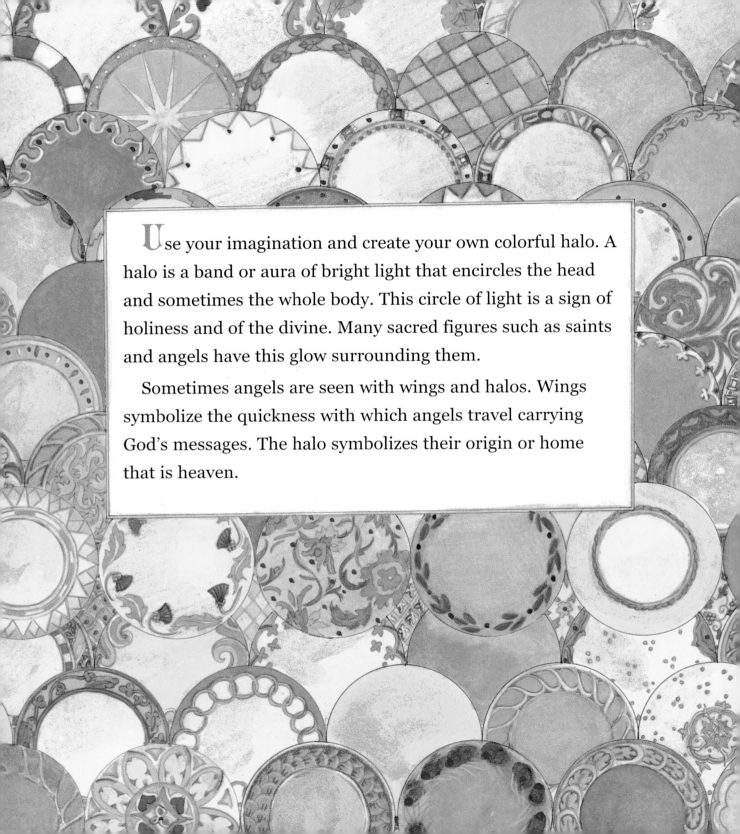

Use your imagination and create your own colorful halo. A halo is a band or aura of bright light that encircles the head and sometimes the whole body. This circle of light is a sign of holiness and of the divine. Many sacred figures such as saints and angels have this glow surrounding them.

Sometimes angels are seen with wings and halos. Wings symbolize the quickness with which angels travel carrying God's messages. The halo symbolizes their origin or home that is heaven.

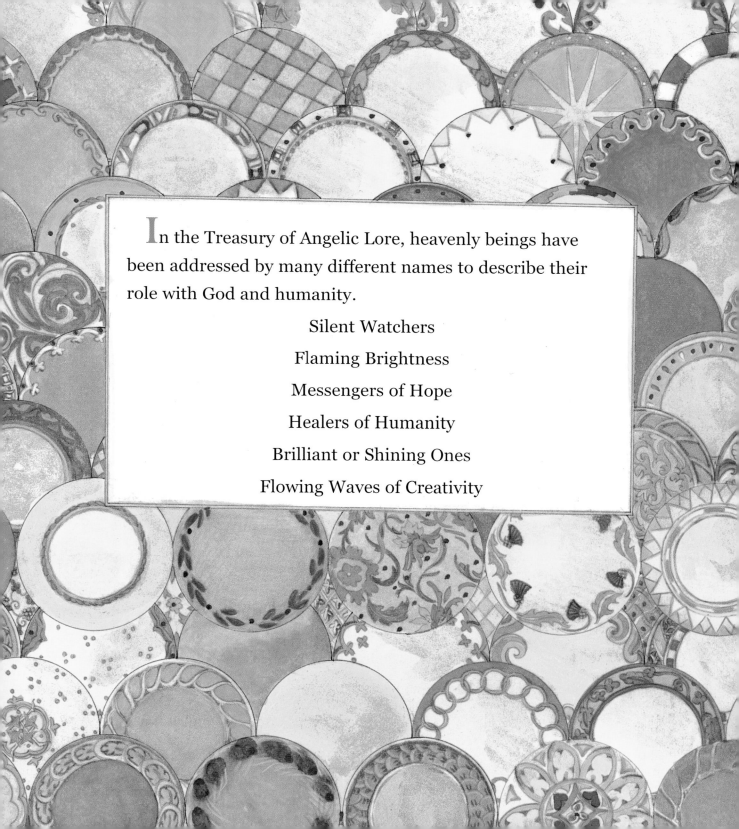

In the Treasury of Angelic Lore, heavenly beings have been addressed by many different names to describe their role with God and humanity.

Silent Watchers

Flaming Brightness

Messengers of Hope

Healers of Humanity

Brilliant or Shining Ones

Flowing Waves of Creativity

When you are feeling sick or unhappy, call on the Angel Heart Doctor. Imagine the angel is making a house call and is repairing your heart to make you feel better. Let the Angel Heart Doctor give you a dose of cheery medicine, such as:

Don't give up.

We like you just as you are.

Everything is going to be okay.

Soon your pain will be gone and you will be filled with warmth, love and light.

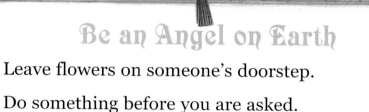

Be an Angel on Earth

- Leave flowers on someone's doorstep.

- Do something before you are asked.

- Smile at everybody. Let them wonder why.

- Hug an adult. You know they could use one.

- Whisper in someone's ear and remind them an angel is over their shoulder.

- Write love notes and leave them for others to discover.

- Take a teddy bear, give it lots of hugs, and then give it to a person who might need a friend.

- Make a halo out of flowers and give it to someone who is especially nice.

Angels are approached
in only one way –

Love

The more you love yourself and the more you love others, the more you will be in the company of angels.

When the lights are out and you are having a hard time falling asleep, start counting angels. See how many you can count. Imagine what each angel is wearing, what color and shape they are, how they move, and what they have to say.

ell yourself before you go to bed that you are going to remember your dreams. Angels bring us special messages in our sleep. In the morning, lie quietly for a moment and try to recall the detail of your dream. Then share your dream with a parent or a special friend. Know that all dreams, even the scary ones, are good. At night, we can work out our fears so our days are filled with joy. Dreams are part of God's plan, and some dreams are gateways to divine ideas sent by your Guardian Angel.

Sleep well.

Guardian Angel Reminders

Have Fun

Play Music

Say a Prayer

Make a Friend

Wear your Halo

Believe in Yourself

Spread your Wings

Give Something Away

Cry when you Need To

𝔄lways remember you have a Guardian Angel to guide, love and protect you throughout life. Open your Wonder Window to the world of wonder and awe.

Wonder Window Series

A collection of timeless books that are a treasury of soul wisdom,
making them fine gifts for all ages.

Other books in the Wonder Window Series:

My Fairy Godmother, an entertaining and
imaginative book that takes you into the realm of
fairies. A Fairy Godmother appears in the
Wonder Window to help you discover the
beauty, love and spirit in every living creature.

My Magical Mermaid, a mesmerizing
book that journeys into the mysteries of the seas.
A Magical Mermaid arrives in the Wonder
Window sharing the gifts of the sea, the
treasures on earth and the magic in life.

BelleTress Books